The Queens Project

by Ivy Infinite Milam

THE QUEENS PROJECT

© 2017 by Ivy Infinite Milam

ISBN 978-0-9993056-1-4 print

First Edition

Photographs and Text by Ivy Infinite Milam
Cover designed by Ivy Infinite Milam
Edited by Jasmin Williams
Layout by Susan Bond

Printed in the United States of America

TABLE OF CONTENTS

PROLOGUE

The Burden of Legacy

I am willing to be undone that I may become the best of who I am.

Legacy is about inheritance. It means a thing passed down, however, not everything inherited is worth taking. I've learned that the legacy you are offering your beloved should reflect the highest of your endowments. As the indigenous would say, it should ensure a continued rich crop that is intended to support, at minimum, the next seven generations to come.

At this time, the world is facing a great challenge on many fronts, calling our attention, so that we may look again. Look again at what we have collectively and individually chosen for ourselves. We have an opportunity to ask ourselves, "Which seeds that have been planted bring a nourishing harvest, and what is a spoiled crop?" "What do we have that we should be grateful for, and what must be transformed?" This is our true work.

The Queens Project is about the legacy of ALL people. It is Ethno-Autobiographical in nature but reserves a universal kinship. It is about our inheritance and what we choose to make of it. I encourage all people to refute the negative popular culture caricature of the black woman. Instead, we should be reminded of her value and tremendous contributions throughout the world's history. Until all of society understands that we belong to one another in a shared greatness, we cannot reach our highest potential. My work is to acknowledge the identity of black women as Queens, reminding them of their unshakable, unapologetic, courageous, empowered and worthy selves.

The Queens Project has become my living prayer. My understanding of prayer is that it is best approached as an offering of one's self or a conversation, versus a request. Prayer at its best is a response to the Divine, knowing our inquiries have already been answered far before we have sourced the question. What is required while in prayer is gratitude and a deep listening for further instruction. The answer to the prayer is in our response. The Queens Project is my response to the questions of; what Legacy will we build upon? It is about the power of identity. It is my service and my conversation with the Divine through the mediums of photographic art, collective wisdom, and storytelling.

INTRODUCTION

Bless the elders for they have come a long way.
Bless the children for they have a long way to go.
Bless those in between for they are doing the good work.
-African Proverb

My relationship with the concepts of legacy and inheritance began early in life.
As a young girl, I wanted to know about my lineage, my purpose, and role in the world. I believed that by gathering and applying collective wisdom to my life, I would better develop as a person, and I would gain valuable tools to share that would inspire, uplift and empower others.

This mindset has stayed with me over the years, and I continue to apply myself as a coach, artist, writer, educator, and community advocate. The Queens Project brings together some of my various gifts and passions in a way that serves the greater good. Before I speak on that, I must first address the salient themes that developed from this project: The power of Oral Tradition, Cross-Cultural Bridging (through stories), Symbolism in Art and Imagery, Empowerment and Esteem, Identity and Legacy.

At age fourteen I began a journey of exploration that led me to powerful learning experiences from many leaders, teachers, and healers around the world. I traveled to engage with other cultures, seeking a common thread. I wanted to know how it is that communities and individuals could truly thrive; living out joyous, empowered, healthy and positive lives. I received many answers to these questions. I found them in the teachings of indigenous communities, in the wisdom of elders, in the insight of gurus, priests, and artists.

During this exploration, I discovered two things to be true: All people are shaped by what they witness, and all people are shaped by being witnessed. I began to realize the importance and the role of the Oral Tradition of storytelling and the transformational power of the images we see and what people see in us.

THE POWER OF STORY, THE STORY IN ART

Stories matter. They win or lose elections. They land jobs. They scare us or they give us hope. They can harm. They can help. Stories and images can change our perception of ourselves, each other and the world. To illustrate, I'd like to share the following examples:

- An officer uses deadly force against a person that is later deemed to be non-threatening. I believe we should consider the possibility that the officers' reaction to the situation was an authentic one. One of fear and mistrust born from the negative narratives that he had internalized, shaping belief and potentially pre-paving an outcome. In the mind of the officer, there was truly a threat where there wasn't.

- In another instance, there's a racially driven act of hate toward a black person. The act was a choice. Again, we must ask ourselves what beliefs, ideas, and stories where internalized. I wonder what dehumanizing jokes were told around that person's dinner table as a child, what movies were watched that promoted the stereotype of the violent black male or what descriptive language was used regarding the black perpetrator versus the white perpetrator of the five o'clock news?

The same concept can be applied to the images we take in.

- A young girl looks at magazines that have a single representation of beauty. This image does not reflect her view of herself. By way of deductive reasoning, she unconsciously or consciously concludes that because she looks nothing like the image of those women, she must be unattractive. In this instance, the image on the magazine has become the symbol of beauty.

Stories can affirm and validate. People create their identities and define social values.

Stories pass down culture. Before written word, there were the oral traditions. Memorizing of stories ensured a passing down of traditions, values, and culture.

Stories are where the imagination and reality meet. Stories can help us visualize different outcomes, try out possible futures for ourselves or reconsider previous experiences. If we see different perspectives, we can better relate to the "difference," of a person. It's called, putting yourself in someone else's shoes.

Stories can heal. Stories can address pain, fear, confusion or anger through a transformative message or a modeling of resolution.

What I want to illustrate here is that words, stories, and images have power. We should be intentional when we use them. They are Symbols. In the context of this book, I offer the definition of the Symbol as follows; A symbol is a mark, character or object that ignites our associative thinking at the levels of both the conscious and unconscious mind.

Carl Jung states, "The symbol is the mechanism to transform the unconscious mind."

THE QUEENS PROJECT

My mentor would say "leave the space better than you found it." I apply that to all of life.

In 2004 I traveled to Accra, Ghana, where names are more complex. People introduced themselves as Mary or Mark, their "Christian name." I later learned that they also had a tribal name, family name, even a common name based on the day of the week they were born. It was common that you were given a name that connected you to your family legacy and your purpose in life. When you went through rites of passage or life initiations, a name could choose you. The name itself tells a story, gives divine purpose and power to your mission. I envied this frank acknowledgement of growth.

With that experience in mind, I've entitled this work, The Queens Project, because the women I chose to interview, represent and embody the character qualities of the Archetypal Queen.

Positive Qualities of the Archetypal Queen:

- Vision & Intuition
- Influence
- Grace
- Striking Appearance and Presence
- Leadership

- Sacred Mother- Creative and Nurturing
- Protector
- Excellence
- Justice
- Self-Expression
- Will
- Power
- Service
- Personal Wellness
- Spiritual Warriorship

The Queens Project contains portraiture that depicts Black American women in the Pacific Northwest as their Alter Egos, their embodied highest representation of self. They are authentic examples of the diverse, luminous experience of the Black American spectrum. Each woman has offered a story, leaving her imprint and positive impact as a gift to communities. It has been a high honor to get to know, interview and photograph each woman.

VISION BOARD: A TRANSFORMATIONAL TOOL

This material is a tool for reflection. It is a reminder of what we have inherited and what we will choose our legacy to be. Its message connects us to our world view, cross-cultural relationships and personal success. It addresses false internalized beliefs & affirms greatness, challenging negative stereotypes perpetuated by popular culture.

Use this book as a tool. Search for ways you can relate to, be affirmed, or inspired by its contents.
The last pages of this book are about you and your Queendom or Kingdom! There are pages dedicated to YOU as the visionary. The pages provided offer space for your Vision Board. You can tell your story, define who you are, and create what your legacy will be. The Vision Board is dedicated to the practice of radical self exceptance and love, and manifesting the life dream. The Alter Ego is THE HIGHEST EMBODIMENT of our true selves. It is who we would become if we were FEARLESS; unafraid of judgement, success, loss, change and challenge. With this mindset, I encourage you to close your eyes, clear your mind and allow inspiration to guide you in the creation of your best you.

Create your TODAY story. Create a collage, art, or place an image of yourself, alongside your story about your life dreams. Acknowledge your present gifts and talents, and aspirations. Speak to the ways you are successful.

Create your TOMORROW story. Create a collage, art, or place an image of yourself alongside your story from the perspective of the future you, ten years in the future. What have you achieved, who have you become, what ways have you given back and what did you overcome?

Create your FOREVER story. Create a collage with art or images alongside your story that relates to the legacy you'll leave behind.

See Pages 32-34

Aramis Hamer
Artist, Spiritual Being, Community Advocate
Business(es): AOHAMER

ARAMIS HAMER
Alter Ego… OCTAVIA

I've thought about how powerful struggle can be, and how powerful rock bottom can really propel you to do something great. Three years ago, I was at a rock bottom place where my whole mental state was unstable. I was in the hospital. I experienced a car accident. I was transitioning through jobs. Literally, everything that could have went wrong, went wrong. I became very depressed to the point where I was on medication. I was wallowing in that state for a long time. I don't know what snapped in me, but there was a moment where I realized nobody is going to make me be better or change unless I take steps to do it. From there, I set a serious intention to take full control of my life. We, as spiritual beings having this physical experience, we have so much power beyond what we are told, shown, or educated about. When you tap into that, you can do unbelievable things. I needed to embrace this godliness, this God that is within all of us, and not God from the state of religious doctrine, but this manifestation of a supreme being that's within us. I got to the place of pulling myself up from every single end… mind, body, spirit, and finances. I started working out, and I lost 15 pounds. I started being more consistent with my finances, checking my account regularly and paying my bills. I began to do simple adult things that I didn't want to do before and taking full control of my life. From my meditation practice, as an artist, and as a creator, I have so many ideas with a lot going on. I feel so much for the world and people in general. Before, I was like, this world is very depressing--depending on what angle you look at it. When I started to tap more into meditation practice, which is a beautiful state to view the world with whatever lens I deem most beautiful. I also tried to create a more beautiful world through art, through being more kind to people. I was amazed because I could do anything. It comes with a level of awareness that takes cultivation, discipline, intention and time. I wish somebody told me that I don't have to be as "pretty" as the Instagram models and I don't have to have a million dollars by twenty-one. Sometimes it's about putting those blinders on and just living your truth with no other distractions.

Imani Simms
Performance Artist, Poet, Facilitator, Curator,
Educator
Business(es): Imani Simms

IMANI SIMMS
Alter Ego… IMANI SIMMS

As a kid, I always felt like I was an outsider because I was quirky. I was nerdy in a sense because I really loved to read science fiction. I loved other worlds, fantasy, and myths. I didn't have friends who understood that world. I had to find my own way to express myself through the mediums I enjoyed. I took to acting because that enabled me to embody another character. That fulfilled my need to be in another world. What I would say to folks or youth is, fully acknowledge your wholeness and your very layered existence. I found that growing up black in Seattle; I was always called an Oreo because my dad was adamant about me sounding educated and my mom was really excited about me being a lady. I didn't find the truth of me until I started to intersect those ideas. I'm very self-identified, but I'm also suburban, quirky, queer, black, and woman. It wasn't until my mid-20s that I started to connect those circles and find a place for safety, where I could be my whole self. Seattle makes that difficult, but I found a few pockets that encourage those multi-layered aspects of myself. I think the most important thing is to let that freak flag fly. A lot of us feel like weirdos, and I want to de-stigmatize the word weirdo. I think everyone has their own way of showing up in the world and none of that is weird.

Abiola Akanni… "means born into wealth."
Yoga Instructor, Creator of Trap Vinyasa
Business(es): Yoga by Biola

ABIOLA AKANNI
Alter Ego… ABIOLA AKANNI

Self-awareness was one of the first things that my yoga practice gave me. I started to see the decrepit thoughts that I had about myself which allowed me to see the lack of self-love I had or more of a self-hate. Self-awareness was essential because I think we are fearful of seeing and examining ourselves. The second thing was empowerment. I started to feel empowered through my practice. It started out physically; my body started to change. I also started to feel empowered by what I was uncovering internally. My self-awareness was allowing me to see what I believed about myself, my life, and the people around me. I was vanquishing those things, and I was able to change those beliefs and internally changed my reality. The physicality empowered me as well. The third one was discipline. I always had a negative connotation to discipline. I was heavily disciplined when I was younger, much more than my siblings. I'm a Nigerian American, and my parents are from Nigeria. Obviously, each child is different. I was a very peculiar child and had a very sour taste in my mouth when it came to discipline. Towards the end of my yoga practice, I started to see the benefits of training. I think it helped me to transcend how I saw discipline and reacquaint myself with control in a way that held a space for me while providing order. Not necessarily structure and a syringe in a hard way but it provided the order that held a safe space for me in the way I needed. I started to acquire self-love which was the fourth self-healing benefit, and I never learned that before. I don't blame my parents for that. Who knows if when my parents were growing up if self-love was even a thing? I started to fall in love with myself or grow in love with myself, and as a result, the divinity inside of me became more aware of who I was in God, who I was as someone with a Christian background. So, who I am in Christ but also the divinity of that, I felt so much enlightenment in that definition of who God is beyond biblical terms. To have a relationship with God through self-love, ultimately that led me to Samadhi which means blissful, oneness with God.

Joyce Hosea
Entrepreneur, Chef
Business(es): The Melding Pot (Commercial Kitchen)

JOYCE HOSEA
Alter Ego… JOYCE HOSEA

I was born and raised in Washington State. I can remember being a determined, four-year-old child. I would ask my mother to pull over on the side of the road whenever I'd see a small Volkswagen Beetle. I would get so excited! "Can I pick it up? Can I pick it up?" I would say. The answer was always, "No, you can't lift that car. It's too heavy." After my relentless pitches to my mother, she finally gave in and pulled over to a baby blue Volkswagen Beetle. She stood beside me and told me to try and lift it. Of course, with much determination, I was unable to move it. It was a sad evening, but what I started to say to myself at that age was, "I can do it!". Which is my life mantra to this day. My mother realized a valuable lesson from my determination... to always try and encourage me. There may be some difficult obstacles but don't let that deter your goals.

I have taken the road less traveled to get to where I'm at today, whether working several low wage jobs to learn a skill or being in my late forties and one of the oldest enrolled in culinary school. I do everything with intention, and I always ask myself, what am I doing right now, is it going to make me happy and whole at the end? If I can answer "yes," then I keep going in that direction.

BERI GEBREHIWOT
Entrepreneur, Mother
Business(es): Her Big Day, Habesha Moms Project

BERI GEBREHIWOT
Alter Ego… WARRIOR PRINCESS

My culture is unique because I've grown up in so many different cultures and environments--coming here to America with my parents when I was just seven years old. My parents fled Eritrea from a thirty-year war. I was born in Sudan. I am the oldest of six kids. My initial or original culture of being is an Eritrean woman or a young Eritrean girl and then being dropped off into this foreign place with a whole different culture. My parents adjusted to America and I, of course, adjusted much quicker than they did. As a young girl absorbing everything around me--with that came wanting to become that new culture. I went to school or hung out with friends, and at home, I was strictly Eritrean, because my parents put all kinds of restrictions on what we could watch, what we could wear, how we did our hair, who we talked to and, the language that was spoken at home. They were very restrictive. It was for them, out of fear, and wanting to preserve culture and heritage, but it also did a disservice because it didn't show me how to be Eritrean and proud of it, in ways I could share it with the world or with my American friends. It was more rebellious restrictive; I was told how to live and who to be. I immediately wanted to turn that off and just be this other person outside our home. It was a big culture clash between us that went on until literally after high school.

After graduating, we went on our first family trip to Eritrea and everything just kind of came back full circle for me. I felt more at home and at peace with my identity and who I was. Surrounded by an entire country of people who looked like me, individuals who shared my identity and culture felt wonderful. What we ate, how we dressed, the different roles and expectations seemed to be the same. Having "real cousins," not people we called cousins because they were Eritrean in the states. Meeting people who were related to me by blood, like my four grandparents. That trip to Eritrea solidified who I truly was, and gave me permission to be me, even when we came back to the states.

Jade Solomon Curtiss
Choreographer, Dance Artist, Founder of Solo Magic
Business(es): Solo Magic

JADE SOLOMON CURTIS
Alter Ego… JADE SOLOMON CURTIS

Right now, I am more interested in exploring what's happening deep down in me. I'm interested in exploring the conversations I'm having with people and exploring, showing work or rather creating work that reflects the current state of my existence, and that is not always pretty.

Debrena Jackson Gandy
Best-Selling Author, Award Winning Leader & Speaker, Transformational Success Coach, Relationship Expert
Business(es): The Million Dollar Mentor
Books: The Love Lies, Sacred Pampering Principles, All the Joy You Can Stand

DEBRENA JACKSON GANDY
Alter Ego… JUICY MANIFESTRESS

The Juicy Life is the life lived by a JUICY WOMAN. A Juicy Woman's spirit is filled with "sweet joy juice," and she experiences fulfillment in every area of her life. The Juicy Life is one lived from a sacred self-caring consciousness, where you relate to your body as a divine living temple, your level of thinking is based upon holistic success, and your life generates an experience of deep joy, deep peace, ease, prosperity, and flow.

The Juicy Life is a highly passionate and sensuous life that is stimulating mentally, emotionally, spiritually and aesthetically. You are flowing in your gifts, and your talents, skills, and abilities are fully engaged and "in play." When you are living a Juicy Life, you don't covet the life of others, nor wish you had someone else's life, things, man, money or body. Instead, the life you've designed and are living is pleasing to you. You recognize that you are a powerful and creative being, with the ability to be the Chief Design Officer of your life.

You cherish silence, stillness, and solitude, and you have a Daily Prayer and Meditation practice for divine communication and communion time with God. You make time to intimately connect with God daily because you understand and highly value the profound benefits and results of taking time each morning to tap into and tune into the love, joy, blessings and divine wisdom plentifully available to you.

The JUICY LIFE is a deeply rewarding life of order, beauty, joy and deep satisfaction.

Lataunya Witherspoon
Founder of SpoonFed Training, Educator,
Coach, American Ninja Warrior Competitor
Business(es):SpoonFed Training

LATAUNYA WITHERSPOON
Alter Ego… ROYAL WARRIOR

I have experience with mentoring many young women and young girls. In most cases, many of them struggle with self--being very insecure about themselves. Whether they are insecure because they came from different backgrounds where it's very challenging for them, no one told them they could make it, and or that they can graduate from high school. So, I truly feel like it's important that you surround yourself with the right people. If you're around people who are very negative most of the time then quite naturally that's going to rub off on you. You're not even going to know it, but subconsciously in your mind, you've already brainwashed yourself into believing that you can't do something. So, whenever I'm mentoring youth, I'm always telling them how important it is to encourage themselves. Find something, whatever your faith is, and really try to dig down deep and understand that you can do it. I always think about our ancestors--everything they had to go through. The stuff we had to go through doesn't even compare. We must dig down and find that something that will keep us going and then just go after it. You have got to find something that you love, you are passionate about and try to master that.

Keisha Credit
Entrepreneur, Wig Designer
Business(es): Lucke by Keisha Custom Wig Making,
Super Lit Apparel, Egocentric

KEISHA CREDIT
Alter Ego… LUCKE

I'm a wig maker. My previous career was at Microsoft. However, I decided to leave Microsoft to pursue my passion, which was doing different styles with my hair. I am not a trained hairdresser--everything was self-taught. Eventually business just kind of took off, and I got too busy to do both. I took a leap of faith and said--you know what--I'm going to follow my heart and step away from Microsoft in Seattle, which was like crazy because everyone's trying to scratch like nails and teeth to get in there and here I was leaving--that was three years ago. Since then I've started two other companies, one is focused on hair care products, and another one is centered around Christian apparel. Now, I'm transitioning my career and my focus into helping other entrepreneurs pursue their passions, take that leap of faith and share their transparent story. Many times, people think--Oh my gosh you work for yourself--that is awesome, and I'm like--no, there are some days when this is just crazy. So, I'm trying to tell my story, encourage others and help them take that step. I think more people should do it. We need more chiefs. I feel like why not us? I think especially within the community of color that we are afraid. We were raised to believe--you go to school to get a job versus you go to school to follow your dream. Often when we hear follow your dream, you think that you have to be poor, which is not the case at all, where as in other communities, following your dream means being a CEO, running a company, having employees, etc. My goal is to change the dialogue around what it means to be an entrepreneur, tell the transparent story, and get the next generation to believe in themselves to the point that it is mind-blowing.

Sheley Secrest
Attorney, Activist, NAACP Leader, Mother
Business: Law Offices of Sheley Secrest

SHELEY SECREST
Alter Ego… Sheley Secrest

There's such a strong community here in Seattle that can reach our children where others can't. You've got Dr. Maxine Mimms, who is an educator, who says, "before you kick them out of an alternative school, send them to me." I want to make sure that we're investing in leaders like Mimms. Crime has decreased over the last ten years by sixty percent. That's huge! That should tell all lawmakers--stop building jails, stop hiring more police officers, and stop building more police precincts. Invest in the community that's able to reach our children, because we are and we are making it on the broken pieces. We're saving our children, we are bringing in the jobs, and we're making it work, but we're not doing it with city resources. That is unacceptable to me. That's another reason why I'm standing on every single corner throughout Seattle saying—hey there's a different way. You need to fund the work that folks in the community have been doing because it is work. We are trying to make sure that we're putting in the resources to help the community.

Takiyah Jackson
Master of Education, Director of African American
Development at UC Berkeley, Founder of Kindtagious
Seattle, Community Advocate, Member of the Wash-
ington State Executive Branch of Government.
Business(es): Kindtagious Seattle

TAKIYAH JACKSON
Alter Ego… KILOLO

What I would say to youth is never let societal norms and traditions limit your thinking, options, and opportunities in life. Traditional standards try to keep you in the boxes that have been arranged for gender, sexuality, race, identity, age, ability and beyond. Society tries to force you to pick boxes so they can keep you in them and convince you to prescribe to the norms they have assigned to those boxes. So, if you don't understand how to live out your own freedom and you don't know what you stand for, someone is going to tell you who you should be and you will be on the path they see for you instead of the path you see for yourself.

All my life, people have tried to limit my options with societal norms, but it did not work. I have always thought outside of all boxes which have been hard for people around me who were stuck in those boxes. I always ignored and pushed back against the boundaries people tried to put on me. When I was seven years old, I wanted to play football on an all-boys team, so I signed up. Although there were no official rules stating that football was restricted to boys, many people would say to me, "football is a sport for boys." My reply would always be, "then how am I here playing on the team?"

When I was nine years old, a similar situation happened when I wanted to join a race team for downhill skiing. I often heard from many people say, "skiing is not for black people," and again I would reply, "then how am I on a race team for skiing?"

I have learned that people reject things they don't understand, and they don't understand because they rely on societal norms and traditions to shape their thoughts about what is expected and accepted. I have always felt that anything that limits your thinking, options, and opportunities is unacceptable. I try to deconstruct and dismantle harmful and restrictive thinking, and I aim to empower all people to dream without limits. Growing up, some people were offended that I would not follow the crowd or prescribe to the boxes they were prisoners to, and some still are, but I continue to advocate for people to form their own knowledge and make informed and empowered decisions for your life. Understanding and living out your freedom is the most liberating way of life and the only way of life for me.

Nichelle iNfinity Alderson
MSW, LICSW
Business(es): iNfinitely Well LLC, Holistic Coaching &
Consultation
Alderson & Associates PLLC, Social Work Services.
iNfinity Presents, arts & events

NICHELLE ALDERSON
Alter Ego… LUCI, my purest self.

First, I pray. I say--if it's in God's will and if I had it my way insert dream then I envision it. I daydream and meditate on the absolute ideal version of the unfolding of my dream. I envision myself already having arrived at the destination, goals accomplished and celebrating the arrival. I get excited about it! I make it real in my mind, meaning I create mental images that I can reference back to often to build upon and work towards--in my conscious and subconscious mind. Then I reverse, engineer it. I write down the steps that it took to manifest that dream. Then I get to it. I take the steps and look for mentorship and support to see it through. I talk about it and continue to dream about it--feeding it by doing my part.

Then I trust God. If it is meant to be it will, that I know for sure. It's faith that gives me the patience to take my time and see things through, as well as the confidence in myself to accomplish my wildest dreams!

Kristi Brown
Chef
Business(es): That Brown Girl Cooks

KRISTI BROWN
Alter Ego… CHEF KRISTI BROWN

The lessons I've learned while building the Chef Kristi
Brown legacy…

Drinking water helps me stay fluid in my MIND,
BODY, SPIRIT.

Do you give yourself what you give others?

Yoga helps me stay balanced and know how I'm feeling
in every part of my body.

Not necessarily in this order!

MONIQUE FRANKLIN, accompanied by daughter,
AKILAH FRANKLIN
Alter Ego… Inspired Child

There's this idealism that I live by that I call love, power, and purpose. The idea is you must start with loving and understanding yourself, your community, and the world in which you live. Once you attain that, you reach a level of power that allows you to live out your purpose. Loving yourself and others gives you clarity and energy that allows you to obtain personal power, and the clarity to

discern what your purpose is and then to execute that purpose, to be that purpose in life.

In high school, I failed math twice. In my junior year, for the first time in chemistry, I got to understand what math was for--not as an abstract concept which I had been taught previously, but that math was a tool to un-

Monique Franklin… with daughter Akilah Franklin
Artist, Poet, Scientist, Mother
Business(es): Verbal Oasis, Inspired Child

math, something I had failed. I decided I wanted to make choices based on things that I wanted to do and not about choosing to pursue chemistry because it might have been harder. I decided to go down the chemistry path. I ended up having to pay for classes at the remedial level and work my way up. In doing that, I realized I was missing a fundamental block in learning math, I didn't understand the order of operations, and without that piece makes it difficult to learn math. What I came to understand is that should have been easy for my teacher to identify. I had the same teacher for two years in a row, and she didn't see that. What was illustrated for me are a couple of things: Our capabilities are something we should investigate ourselves. I think as students we blame ourselves when we don't understand things when the blame could be a combination of the teacher and the student. When I learned that, I also realized I didn't have the same levels of experiences with math as I had with reading and writing. Once I gained the same experiences, I was excelling in math at the same level I was excelling in other subjects. That's what brought me down the path of achieving, A's in mathematics and then my Computer Science degree from the University of Washington.

derstand the world and how it works. That was the first time I was taught math in that context. I began to love chemistry and math for that purpose. When I graduated, I had to decide on what I wanted to do in college. I had two paths ahead of me. The path of creative writing which I've been told I'm good at or explore this passion of chemistry which would require me to take

Through my story, we learn that we become good at things that we practice. Things that we practice well. If there's something that you want to do and have never done before or haven't been successful in, in the past, find the tools to practice and gain those skills. If there's something you want in the future, know that you're going to attain that through practice.

NAME:

ALTER EGO:

Create your TODAY story. Create a collogue, create art or place an image of yourself along side a story about your life dreams, acknowledge your present gifts and talents, and aspirations. Speak to the ways you are successful.

...SELF PORTRAIT, COLLOGUE, ART, SYMBOLS

STORY...

NAME:

ALTER EGO:

Create your *TOMORROW* story. Create a collogue, create art or place an image of yourself along side your story from the perspective of the future you , 10 years in the future. What have you achieved, who have you become, what ways have you given back and what did you overcome?

...SELF PORTRAIT, COLLOGUE, ART, SYMBOLS

STORY...

NAME:

ALTER EGO:

Create your FOREVER story. Create a collogue, create art or images along side your story of the legacy you'll leave behind.

...SELF PORTRAIT, COLLOGUE, ART, SYMBOLS

STORY...

ACKNOWLEDGEMENTS

I must first acknowledge my mother, Joyce Hosea, who taught me by example, what it means to be bold, boundless and beautiful. It has been an honor to witness my mother reach her dreams in the face of challenge. I thank you mom for telling me my dreams where possible.

To Tim Burdick, one of the predominant role models in my life, thank you for all the ways you show up for me. I love you dearly.

To my sisters, Breona Milam and Kellie Bendickson for your unshakable forever love, you have been my rock more than I can count.

Jo-Nathan Thomas, we are on this journey together. Thank you for the ways you challenge me to grow, that I may become the best version of myself. Here's to our love and legacy.

I give deep thanks and gratitude to my many mentors, elders, guardians, and guides. For allowing the great mystery to use you in ways that support my journey.

Ashley Rugge, Melia LaCour, R. Rose, Mujale Chisebuka, Reyshard Elsemaj… You have inspired, supported and cheered me on every step of the way. Creating with you and watching you create is pure magic.

To my high school teacher, Peter Suruda. You gave me permission to write. I haven't stopped since.

To my grandmothers, Dr. Gwen Hosea Mimms and Dr. Maxine Mimms, thank you for your guidance and your legacy.

Char Sundust, you have always been an inspiration & will always be a bright light in my life. Knowing you has changed my life beyond measure. You have been a teacher, a guide, a friend, and a constant. Thank you.

A very special thank you to Nancy for her priceless and selfless contribution to this work and mentorship. You are a brilliant photographer and artist. You are an even more incredible person.

I cannot thank the women of the Queens Project enough for all of the magic they have shared with me on this journey.

In closing, without the divine, the creative pulse, the light... how could I accomplish anything? I give thanks to the most high for my life.

QUEENS PROJECT PHOTOGRAPHY TEAM

Infinite Milam- Creative Director, Set Director, Lead Photographer, Graphic Designer

Nancy Adams Treder- Set Director, Lead Photographer

Reyshard Elsemaj- Creative Director, Artist, Hair, Makeup, Stylist Extraordinaire

Mujale Chisebuka- Set Coordinator

QUEENS PROJECT GLAM TEAM

Makeup Artists:

- **Kenya Simpson**
  Akilah, Infinite and Keisha

- **Maritza Mesa**
  Debrena and Monique

- **Andrea Davilah-Pelayo**
  Jade and Nichelle

- **Rosie Hernandez**
  Kristi

Hair Stylists:

- **Sarah Simon**
  Sheley and Lataunya,

- **Anjelic Smith**
  Nichelle and Monique

CPSIA information can be obtained at www.ICGtesting.com
Printed in the USA
LVIW01n2349060318
568945LV00006B/25